Sayings
for
Sufferers

Edited by David C. Jones

Detselig Enterprises Ltd.

Calgary, Alberta, Canada

Canadian Cataloguing in Publication Data

Jones, David C., 1943-
  Sayings for Sufferers

ISBN 1-55059-158-4

1. Suffering—Quotations, maxims, etc. 2. Self-actu-alization (Psychology)—Quotations, maxims, etc.   I. Title.

BF789.S8J64   1997   152.4   C97-910866-7

Detselig Enterprises Ltd.
210, 1220 Kensington Rd. N.W.
Calgary, Alberta T2N 3P5

Detselig Enterprises Ltd. appreciates the financial support for our 1997 publishing program, provided by Canadian Heritage and the Alberta Foundation for the Arts, a beneficiary of the Lottery Fund of the Government of Alberta.

Printed in Canada   ISBN 1-55059-158-4
SAN 115-0324

Cover design by Dean Macdonald

Dedication

To Sathya Sai Baba, Teacher

Introduction

Suffering and Self

What purpose has pain? Learning. Strengthening. The discovery of self and the things that fulfill it. What causes sorrow? Ignorance; worst of all, ignorance of self. And the deadliest of that is self-condemnation – the faith of the faithless – a definition, a blueprint of the self's future, its flaws and traumas, worthlessness and just deserts.

Choose who we are, and we clarify our capabilities; choose, and we set the limits of our accomplishment. Whether the choice be conscious or not is immaterial. It is reflected in our every thought and deed, in every nuance and mannerism, in every minute of our lives.

Kindness, compassion, courage and patience always gratify, and their lack always hurts. Where vices thrive, so does disharmony – when all weather, even a breeze, seems a storm, and when all experience, even the serene, seems an annoyance. One day, the Sun King, Louis XIV, scowled at a lackey who was not quite tardy, "I almost had to wait!"

But if pain mentors, so does joy, and the curriculum of joy teaches gently and affectionately the same deep lessons.

"I am . . . but a traveler of whom you asked the way," said George Bernard Shaw, "and I pointed ahead of myself as well as of you."

David C. Jones

Prologue

When Grief is great enough it cuts down until it finds the very soul, and this is Agony. And he who has it does not seek to share it with another, for he knows that no other human being can comprehend it – it belongs to him alone, and he is dumb. There is a dignity and sanctity and grace about suffering; it holds a chastening and purifying quality that makes a king or queen of him who has it. Only the silence of night dare look upon it, and no sympathy save God's can mitigate it.

Elbert Hubbard

Illness is not something a person has. It's another way of being.

Jonathan Miller

"Swami, what is the root of all chaos and trouble in the world today?" asked a seeker.

He replied, "What we think we do not speak, what we speak we do not act, what we act we do not mean, what we actually mean, we never think about in the first place. What is the world? . . . It is the reflection of your own self. When there is chaos within your own self, how can you find tranquillity outside? Otherwise, everything outside is in perfect harmony. The sun, the moon, the wind, everything follows nature's laws. Only human beings break the laws of nature and suffer. The discontentment and disharmony in one's own self get projected outside as chaos. Set your own Self in order, and you will find everything outside in order."

Sathya Sai Baba

First Principles

God is seated in the hearts of all.

Bhagavad Gita

In every place where you find the imprint of men's feet, there am I.

The Talmud

The kingdom of heaven is within you.

The Bible

God obliges no man more than he has given him ability to perform.

The Koran

However broken down the spirit's shrine, the spirit is there all the same.

Nigerian proverb

Experience is a hard teacher because she gives the test first, the lesson afterwards.

Vernon Sanders Law

Soon or late I know you will see that to do right brings good, and to do wrong brings misery, but you will abide by the law and all good things be yours. I cannot change these laws – I cannot make you exempt from your own blunders and mistakes.

And you cannot change the eternal laws for me, even though you die for me.

Elbert Hubbard

What I gave, I have; what I spent, I had; what I kept, I lost.

Old Epitaph

Happiness is not a reward – it is a consequence.
Suffering is not a punishment – it is a result.

Robert Green Ingersoll

If there was nothing wrong with the world there
wouldn't be anything for us to do.

George Bernard Shaw

All evolutionary creature life is beset by certain *inevitabilities*. Consider the following:

1. Is *courage* – strength of character – desirable? Then must man be reared in an environment which necessitates grappling with hardships and reacting to disappointments.

2. Is *altruism* – service of one's fellows – desirable? Then must life experience provide for encountering situations of social inequality.

3. Is *hope* – the grandeur of trust – desirable? Then human existence must constantly be confronted with insecurities and recurrent uncertainties.

4. Is *faith* – the supreme assertion of human thought – desirable? Then must the mind of man find itself in that troublesome predicament where it ever knows less than it can believe.

5. Is the *love of truth* and the willingness to go wherever it leads, desirable? Then must man grow up in a world where error is present and falsehood always possible.

6. Is *idealism* – the approaching concept of the divine – desirable? Then must man struggle in an environment of relative goodness and beauty, surroundings stimulative of the irrepressible reach for better things.

7. Is *loyalty* – devotion to highest duty – desirable? Then must man carry on amid the possibilities of betrayal and desertion. The valor of devotion to duty consists in the implied danger of default.

8. Is *unselfishness* – the spirit of self-forgetfulness – desirable? Then must mortal man live face to face with the incessant clamoring of an inescapable self for recognition and honor. Man could not dynamically choose the divine life if there were no self-life to forsake. Man could never lay saving hold on righteousness if there were no potential evil to exalt and differentiate the good by contrast.

9. Is *pleasure* – the satisfaction of happiness – desirable? Then must man live in a world where the alternative of pain and the likelihood of suffering are ever-present experiential possibilities.

The URANTIA Book

The greater the mission that is to be performed, the greater are the challenges that will be met. It cannot be any other way.

Silver Birch

The world is a mirror; show thyself in it, and it will reflect thy image.

Arabic proverb

To the jaundiced all things seem yellow.

Anonymous

Everyone thinks of changing the world, but no one thinks of changing himself.

Leo Tolstoy

The keenest sorrow is to recognize ourselves as the sole cause of all our adversities.

Sophocles

[In] the ancient custom of punishing a murderer by chaining him to the dead body of his victim . . . wherever the man went, he had to drag the putrefying corpse — he could not disentangle himself from the result of his evil act. No more horrible punishment could possibly be devised; but Nature has a plan of retribution that is very much akin to it. What more terrible than this: the evil thing you do shall at once become an integral part of what you are.

Elbert Hubbard

Peace of mind is clearly an internal matter. It must begin with your own thoughts, and then extend outward. It is from your peace of mind that a peaceful perception of the world arises.

A Course in Miracles, V2, 51

Change but your mind on what you want to see, and all the world must change accordingly.

Ibid., V2, 236

Once you know yourself, everything else will be automatically clear . . . . Just as the knowledge of a single clay pot is enough to know all about all clay pots, when you know yourself, all else can be known.

Sathya Sai Baba

There is one grand lie – that we are limited. The only limits we have are the limits we believe.

Wayne Dyer

Judge no one. Who knows what hardships others have suffered?

J. Donald Walters

Suffering isn't ennobling, recovery is.

Christiaan N. Barnard

Suffering – Forms and Causes

There is no error greater than that species of self-deception which leads intelligent beings to crave the exercise of power over other beings for the purpose of depriving these persons of their natural liberties. The golden rule of human fairness cries out against all such fraud, unfairness, selfishness, and unrighteousness.

The URANTIA Book

Power takes as ingratitude the writhing of its victims.

Rabindranath Tagore

Why is murder a sin? Because the life that is in you is the same as the life in all beings. To deny anyone the right to live is to deny the reality of that universal life of which you, too, are an expression. Spiritually speaking, then, murder is suicide.

Paramahansa Yogananda

War is, at first, the hope that one will be better off; next, the expectation that the other fellow will be worse off; then, the satisfaction that he isn't any better off; and finally, the surprise at everyone's being worse off.

Karl Kraus

What loneliness is more lonely than distrust?

George Eliot

We crucify ourselves between two thieves: regret for yesterday and fear of tomorrow.

Fulton Oursler

A cynic is not merely one who reads bitter lessons from the past, he is one who is prematurely disappointed in the future.

Sidney Harris

A pessimist is a guy who feels bad when he feels good for fear he'll feel worse when he feels better.

Ted Robinson

There is no more miserable human being than one in whom nothing is habitual but indecision.

William James

Intuition is impotent without decisiveness. When at last the gift or inspiration you have longed for appears, never reject it, for to do so is to reject yourself, your power to attract your wants and needs. Ofttimes the gift is available but a second in eternity, and if you scorn it, your hand will be worse than empty – it will be heaped high with frustration and regret.

DCJ

Nothing equals the importance of the work in the world in which you are actually living. But though the *work* is important, the *self* is not. When you feel important, you lose energy to the wear and tear of ego dignity so that there is little energy left to do the work. Self-importance not work-importance exhausts immature creatures; it is the self element that exhausts, not the effort to achieve.

The URANTIA Book

The most exhausting thing in life is being insincere.

Anne Morrow Lindbergh

The Liar's punishment is not in the least that he is not believed, but that he cannot believe anyone else.

George Bernard Shaw

Who lies for you will lie against you.

Bosnian proverb

If you keep the company of thieves, you will become one.

Kongo proverb

If you try to cleanse others, you will waste away like soap in the process.

Madagascar proverb

If envy was not such a tearing thing to feel, it would be the most comic of sins. It is usually, if not always, based on a complete misunderstanding of another person's position.

Monica Furlong

Bigotry tries to keep truth safe in its hand with the grip that kills it.

Rabindranath Tagore

The slanderous tongue kills three: the slandered, the slanderer, and him who listens to the slander.

The Talmud

There is no one so rich that he does not still want something.

German proverb

When we lose one we love, our bitterest tears are called forth by the memory of hours when we loved not enough.

Maurice Maeterlinck

Anger does as much damage to the vessel it is stored in as it does to anything it is poured upon.

Anonymous

The price of hating other human beings is loving oneself less.

Elderidge Cleaver

Illnesses are caused not so much by the food people eat or the conditions in which they live, but by mental weakness and mental attitudes, prejudices and predilections. Desires, disappointment, despair – they also cause diseases.

Sathya Sai Baba

All sickness comes from separation. When the separation is denied, it goes.

A Course in Miracles, V1, 514

Depression is an inevitable consequence of separation. So are anxiety, worry, a deep sense of helplessness, misery, suffering and intense fear of loss.

Ibid., V2, 63

The deepest need of man is the need to overcome his separateness, to leave the prison of his aloneness.

Erich Fromm

A person remains immature, whatever his age, as long as he thinks of himself as an exception to the human race.

Harry Overstreet

Fear is the worst enemy. Fear corrodes. Fear impedes the channel through which help can come. Fear disturbs the physical, mental and spiritual atmosphere around you. Fear is the enemy of reason. Fear prevents that calmness of outlook and resolution of mind that are your greatest allies in your life.

Silver Birch

The unforgiving mind is full of fear, and offers love no room to be itself; no place where it can spread its wings in peace and soar above the turmoil of the world. The unforgiving mind is sad, without the hope of respite and release from pain. It suffers and abides in misery, peering about in darkness, seeing not, yet certain of the danger lurking there.

The unforgiving mind is torn with doubt, confused about itself and all it sees; afraid and angry, weak and blustering, afraid to go ahead, afraid to stay, afraid to waken or to go to sleep, afraid of every sound, yet more afraid of stillness; terrified of darkness, yet more terrified at the approach of light. What can the unforgiving mind perceive but its damnation?

A Course in Miracles, V2, 210

Warning:

Never eat more than you can lift.

Miss Piggy

Complications in Recovery

Healing will always stand aside when it would be seen as a threat.

A Course in Miracles, V3, 19

No one desires pain. But he can think that pain is pleasure. No one would avoid his happiness. But he can think that joy is painful, threatening and dangerous. Everyone will receive what he requests. But he can be confused indeed about the things he wants; the state he would attain.

Ibid., V2, 462

The hardest thing to believe when you're young is that people will fight to stay in a rut, but not to get out of one.

Ellen Glasgow

There is a pleasure in being mad, which none but madmen know.

John Dryden

Melancholy. The pleasure of being sad.

Victor Hugo

In the adversity of our best friends we often find something which does not displease us.

François de la Rochefoucauld

He who despises himself esteems himself as a self-despiser.

Friedrich Wilhelm Nietzche

He who loves to discount experts will find his pleasure in the dolts he mistrusts – and what greater joy than in the experts who tragically deceive him.

DCJ

She who loves righteous indignation will find much to be indignant about.

DCJ

Middle Age. The time when you'll do anything to feel better, except give up what's hurting you.

Robert Quillen

A habit cannot be tossed out the window; it must be coaxed down the stairs a step at a time.

Mark Twain

The mind unlearns with difficulty what it has long learned.

Seneca

Men will sooner surrender their rights than their customs.

Moritz Guedmann

Perhaps now and then a castaway on a lonely desert island dreads the thought of being rescued.

Sarah Anne Jewett

Nothing is more desirable than to be released from affliction, but nothing is more frightening than to be deprived of a crutch.

James Baldwin

It is dangerous to abandon one's self to the luxury of grief: it deprives one of courage and even the wish for recovery.

H.F. Amiel

He that won't be counseled can't be helped.

Benjamin Franklin

At forty I lost my illusions,
At fifty I lost my hair,
At sixty my hope and teeth were gone,
And my feet were beyond repair.
At eighty life has clipped my claws,
I'm bent and bowed and cracked;
But I can't give up the ghost because
My follies are intact.

E.Y. Harbur

Once during Prohibition I was forced to live for days on nothing but food and water.

W.C. Fields

In 1969 I published a small book on Humility. It was a pioneering work which has not, to my knowledge, been superseded.

Lord Longford

Mad Solutions

No doubt fate would find it easier than I do to relieve you of your illness. But you will be able to convince yourself that much will be gained if we succeed in transforming your hysterical misery into common unhappiness.

Sigmund Freud

The next time I send a dumb sonofabitch to do something, I go myself!

Michael Curtiz

One of the best temporary cures for pride and affection is seasickness; a man who wants to vomit never puts on airs.

Josh Billings

Optimist. A guy who thinks his wife has quit smoking cigarettes when he finds cigar butts around the house.

Anonymous

Cowardice. The surest protection against temptation.

Mark Twain

Owe money to be paid at Easter, and Lent will seem short.

Italian proverb

Show him death, and he'll be content with fever.

Persian proverb

Warning:

You can't talk of the ocean to a well-frog.
                              Chinese proverb

Sane Solutions

Self-inquiry

Self-examination is the first step to self-improvement and peace.

Sathya Sai Baba

Who is the physician? Only the mind of the patient himself.

A Course in Miracles, V3, 17

Healing is the one ability everyone can develop and must develop if he is to be healed.

Ibid., V1, 111

Action

The only cure for grief is action.

George Henry Lewes

As if Principle: If you want a quality, act as if you already had it.

William James

Hope

The human body experiences a powerful gravitational pull in the direction of hope. That is why the patient's hopes are the physician's secret weapon. They are the hidden ingredients in any prescription.

Norman Cousins

Believe that life is worth living, and your belief will help create the fact.

William James

Humor

Humor is an affirmation of dignity, a declaration of man's superiority to all that befalls him.

Romain Gary

Tact

Very nice, but there are dull stretches.
Comte de Rivarol on a two-line poem.

Is forbidden to steal hotel towels, please. If you are not person to do such is please not to read notice.
Room Notice in Tokyo Hotel

Concentration

The least thing upset him on the links. He missed short putts because of the uproar of butterflies in the adjoining meadows.

P.G. Wodehouse

Simple Pleasures

Animals are such agreeable friends – they ask no questions, they pass no criticisms.

George Eliot

The greatest pleasure of a dog is that you may make a fool of yourself with him and not only will he not scold you, but he will make a fool of himself too.

Samuel Butler

Curiosity

The important thing is not to stop questioning. Curiosity has its own reason for existing. One cannot help but be in awe when he contemplates the mysteries of eternity, of life, of the marvelous structure of reality. It is enough if one tries merely to comprehend a little of this mystery every day. Never lose a holy curiosity.

Albert Einstein

Enthusiasm

The key word in all your problems is *enthusiasm*. Become enthused no matter what you are doing, *but do what you can become enthused in*. This is the secret.

Dr. Bernadt

Patience

The best method of solving some entangled problems is to forsake them for a time.
The URANTIA Book

Give wind and tide a chance to change.
Richard E. Byrd

Calm

Only in quiet water do things mirror themselves undistorted. Only in the quiet mind is there adequate perception of the world.

Hans Margollus

Acceptance

Ah! If you only knew what peace there is in accepted sorrow.

Jeanne de la Motte-Guyton

What is resignation? It is putting God between one's self and one's grief.

Anne Sophie Swetchine

Oneness

The sick and the downcast see themselves as separate from the rest of humanity. To help them, never agree with their sad assessment of themselves – for that is to consummate the separation.

DCJ

Friends

No medicine is more valuable, none more efficacious, none better suited to the cure of all our temporal ills than a friend to whom we may turn for consolation in time of trouble – and with whom we may share our happiness in time of joy.

St. Aelred of Rievaulx

Self-Control

The father with the child he abuses, or the mother with hers, or the teachers with theirs, what is to stop them, but themselves? The children cannot do it; neither can the judiciary with its broken, holey net, cast into the teary waters long after the sorrow.

DCJ

Self-Reliance

The only help worth giving is freeing from the need for further help. Repeated help is no help at all. Do not talk of helping another unless you can put him beyond all need of help.

Nisgardatta Maharaj

Forgiveness

The remedy for injuries is not to remember them.
German proverb

Many promising reconciliations have broken down because while both parties came prepared to forgive, neither party came prepared to be forgiven.
Charles Williams

Desirelessness

"If I had no desires," asked a seeker, "wouldn't I lose all motivation, and become a sort of automaton?"

"Many people imagine so," Yogananda replied. "They think they'd have no further interest in life. But that isn't what happens at all. Rather, you find life to be infinitely more interesting.

"Consider the negative aspect of desire. It keeps you forever fearful. 'What if this happens?' you think; or, 'What if that doesn't happen?' You live in a state of anxiety for the future, or of regret for the past.

"Non-attachment, on the other hand, helps you to live perpetually in a state of inner freedom and happiness. When you can be happy in the present, the you have God.

"Desirelessness doesn't rob you of motivation. Far from it! The more you live in God, the deeper the joy you experience in serving Him."

No matter what happens, look at life with non-attachment.

Never let the thought enter your mind that you own anything. Whenever I see someone who needs something of mine more than I do, I gladly give it to him.

Paramahansa Yogananda

Forbearance, Non-violence, Love

You cannot destroy anger by anger, cruelty by cruelty, hatred by hatred. Anger can be subdued only by forbearance; cruelty can be overcome only by nonviolence; hatred yields only to charity and compassion.

Sathya Sai Baba

Meet anger with silence, respectfully, and for lack of fuel the fires of anger will subside.

J. Donald Walters

I can escape from the world I see by giving up attack thoughts. [This] idea . . . contains the only way out of fear that will ever succeed. Nothing else will work; everything else is meaningless.

A Course in Miracles, V2, 34

Service

Nothing makes one feel so strong as a call for help.

George MacDonald

The secret of overcoming depression is useful activity devoted to the welfare of others.

J. Donald Walters

I don't know what your destiny will be, but one thing I know: the only ones among you who will be really happy are those who will have sought and found how to serve.

Albert Schweitzer

Efforts to serve must spring from agony at the suffering of others, and the service must be the genuine effort to get rid of that anguish. And ... do not worry about the result. Help as much as you can, as efficiently as you can, as silently as you can, as lovingly as you can. Leave the rest to God, who gave you the chance to serve.

Service should not be exhibitionistic; you must seek no reward, not even gratitude or thanks from the recipients.

Sathya Sai Baba

Persistence

Nothing in the world can take the place of persistence. Talent will not; nothing is more common than unsuccessful men of talent. Genius will not; unrewarded genius is almost a proverb. Education will not; the world is full of educated derelicts. Persistence and determination alone are omnipotent.

Calvin Coolidge

Courage

Real self-confidence can never be yours without the exercise of courage.

DCJ

Don't complain at perceived misfortune. Whining only tests other people's patience. Courage in the face of adversity, on the other hand, wins universal admiration.

J. Donald Walters

The choice is up to you. It can either be, "Good morning, God!" or "Good God, morning."

Wayne Dyer

Blessings of Error, Difficulty, Sorrow

Most of what a mortal would call providential is not; his judgment of such matters is very handicapped by lack of farsighted vision into the true meanings and the circumstances of life. Much of what a mortal would call good luck might really be bad luck; the smile of fortune that bestows unearned leisure and undeserved wealth may be the greatest of human afflictions; the apparent cruelty of a perverse fate that heaps tribulation upon some suffering mortal may in reality be the tempering fire that is transmuting the soft iron of immature personality into the tempered steel of real character.

The URANTIA Book

In selecting environment, do not pick one too propitious, otherwise you will plant your roses in muck, when what they demand for exercise is a little difficulty in way of a few rocks to afford anchor for roots. Genius grows only in an environment that does not fully satisfy, and the effort to better the environment and bring about better conditions is exactly the one thing that evolves genius.

Elbert Hubbard

Contentment is the smother of invention.
Ethel Watts Mumford

All progress grows out of discontent with things as they are: discomfort, disgust, displeasure, dissatisfaction, disease.

D. Kenneth Winebrenner

We learn wisdom from failure much more than success. We often discover what WILL do, by finding out what will NOT do.

Samuel Smiles

Insight is oft the lesson of error.

DCJ

A man who has not passed through the inferno of his own passions has never overcome them.

Carl Jung

Character cannot be developed in ease and quiet. Only through experience of trial and suffering can the soul be strengthened, vision cleared, ambition inspired, and success achieved.

Helen Keller

Heaven sends us misfortunes as a moral tonic.

Lady Marguerite Blessington

Tears are often the telescope by which men see far into heaven.

Henry Ward Beecher

Generally, man seeks only happiness and joy; under no stress will he desire misery and grief! He treats happiness and joy as his closest well-wishers and misery and grief as his direct enemies.

This is a great mistake. When one is happy, the risk of grief is great; fear of losing the happiness will haunt man. Misery prompts inquiry, discrimination, self-examination and fear of worse things that might happen. It awakens you from sloth and conceit. Happiness makes one forget one's obligations to oneself as a human being. It drags man into egoism and the sins that egoism leads one to commit. Grief renders man alert and watchful! So misery is a real friend; happiness spreads out the stock of merit and arouses the baser passions. So it is really an enemy.

Sathya Sai Baba

For merit there is a recompense in sneers, and a benefit in sarcasms, and a compensation in hate; for when these things get too pronounced a champion appears.

Elbert Hubbard

The greater the obstacle, the more glory in overcoming it.

Molière

Warning:

Before we can transcend limitations, whether in our own nature or in the circumstances around us, we must try to understand what it is that they are meant to teach.

Every premature withdrawal from the battle of life, merely because it involves stress and strain which we think is too much for us, fails to fulfil the object with which we have entered that battle.

N. Sri Ram

Epilogue

You may be surrounded with small enemies and be retarded by many obstacles, but the big things and the real things of this world and the universe are on your side.

The URANTIA Book

Always affirm inwardly, "I am ageless. I am eternal. I live in timelessness. I was created before the galaxies were formed."

Paramahansa Yogananda

No individual can ultimately fail. The Divinity which descends into humanity is bound to regain its original state.

N. Sri Ram

How can you know whether you chose the stairs to Heaven or the way to hell? Quite easily. How do you feel? Is peace in your awareness?

A Course in Miracles, V1, 460

Printed in November 1997 by

VEILLEUX
ON DEMAND PRINTING INC.

in Boucherville, Quebec